CHEAP MOTELS OF MY YOUTH

George Bilgere

Rattle | *Studio City, California* | *2024*

ISBN: 978-1-931307-56-7

First edition

rattle

Rattle Foundation
12411 Ventura Blvd
Studio City, CA 91604
www.rattle.com

CONTENTS

ACKNOWLEDGMENTS

Grateful acknowledgment is made to *New Ohio Review* for publishing "Nine," "Front Page," and "Insult to Injury," and *Quill & Parchment* for publishing "Market Basket" and "I Heard a Fly Buzz."

CHEAP

MOTELS

OF MY YOUTH

Where are you, gaze of exaltation?
Everything's boredom without you.
—Adam Zagajewski

Nine

I am standing by the pop machine
at the gas station, drinking a root beer.
It cost a dime, my whole allowance.
My bike—a J.C. Higgins three-speed—
looks cool: I just washed it
and waxed the blue fenders.
Grown-ups are moving around me
in kind of a fog. Actually I feel sorry
for grown-ups, with their neckties,
their dark jackets and serious talk.
I am wearing low-top Keds.
Their shoes are hard and gigantic.
Try climbing a tree in those shoes.
How am I supposed to know
that an old, white-haired guy,
a grown-up, is watching me
from his desk in the future,
writing down every move I make.
Why would anybody even do that?
If there's one thing I don't like
it's writing. Writing and division.
This root beer is actually excellent.
It's a hot day. My fenders are waxed.

Matchbook

When the last smoker
has smoked
the last cigarette
I'm going to miss
that deft,
back-handed,
loose-wristed wave,
the two or three
quick snaps
whereby
they put out their match.
How it flared and died
into a smoky elegy.

Because
the young woman
over there,
lighting up,
just did that
magician's trick
to conjure my father
from fifty years away.
He takes a deep,
glorious drag, then
looks back down
at his newspaper
and vanishes
into whatever it is
the dead
are reading about these days.

I Heard a Fly Buzz

I stumbled out into the kitchen,
got the coffee maker started,
did the dishes from last night,
and then you came out in your robe,
wondering why I was up so early,
and I realized I'd misread the clock,
I'd actually gotten up at 7, not 8,
and suddenly I had a whole hour
bestowed upon me by the gods
who dole out our span of time.

And this was long ago, years ago, but
I still have that hour, I've guarded it
zealously, and when the time comes
and the darkness is closing in, and perhaps
I even hear a fly buzz—I'll take out
that hour from the secret place
where I keep it, I'll show it to all of you
gathered around my bedside
and I'll cry out, Look! Another hour!

And that fly will pause in its
goddam buzzing, and all of you—
and that means *you*, Michael and Alex—
all of you will be forced to smile
and say, Really? That's just awesome!

And I shall continue with my reminiscences.

Market Basket

The grocery store where for forty years
my mother shopped, the big old down
at the heels Market Basket with the palm trees
shading the parking lot where she cursed
for decades the slow incompetent parkers,
who cursed her in turn, the Market
Basket whose wide linoleum aisles
she plied with so many barges groaning
with Cheerios and pork chops and milk,
Rice-a-Roni and Hamburger Helper,
Band-Aids and Kool-Aid and Gallo wine,
that cool dim cave where my friends
were bag boys and stock boys
and the first girl I ever dated
was a cashier I took out after her
night shift into the parking lot,
liberating her from that crisp white
Market Basket blouse in the front seat
of my mother's Oldsmobile on summer nights
that smelled of lilac—dear God,
that very Market Basket demolished
in a single day by demented backhoes,
and all its meats and pickles gone,
along with the freezer aisle, so cool
on blazing afternoons in July,
and the racks of Milky Ways and Mars Bars
gone, the bright red Coke machine gone,
and the ancient palomino rocking horse
next to the entrance, where for a nickel
the children of our town galloped
through their childhood,
has galloped away.

Emergency

This is an emergency. That is,
there's an emergency going on
over there, in the corner booth
of this roadside diner somewhere
in western Missouri or is it
Kansas. On the way to California.
It's a little hard to make out
at this distance, but
the emergency involves the woman
sitting with her three children.
She's holding a menu and calculating
prices. California is a long way off,
which is part of the emergency,
as is the divorce still burning
out of control in St. Louis. Only
yesterday she drove away
from the house, her life,
her friends, the Mason jars
full of cracked ice and Jim Beam
her husband, her *ex-husband,*
swam through every night like
some kind of prehistoric fish. The kids
are coloring, nice of the waitress
to bring them crayons. Crayons seem
impossible now, they won't
get her to California with her kids—
that's part of the emergency—where
maybe there will be a life, but first
she must order two club sandwiches,
the girls can split one, the boy
needs a whole club sandwich,
I still like them, even today, and nothing
for herself.

Dave

At the start of summer, Dave begins
building his screened-in porch.
Dave, retired from teaching
Special Ed. Forty years, maybe two
thousand, three thousand kids, somewhat
broken, connections frayed. First,
the concrete foundation.
A divorce in the background, still
festering. June was flooring,
mortise and tenon. The wood's
anguish on the table saw.
July on the ladder, small arms fire
of nail gun and the silhouette
of Dave up there, godly among
the embassies of the clouds.
His drinking in abeyance.
Dave lordly with his tool belt,
straw boater shielding his baldness,
Dave with a hammer
and a tuna fish sandwich
astride the neighborhood.
August was framing and electric,
and three wooden steps ascending
from the sea of grass. Sweet
paint, white as cream, the denouement.
Two, maybe three thousand kids.
You can tell me about Napoleon,
William the Conqueror. You can talk
about Charlemagne and Alexander
the Great. And you can talk
about Dave, robed in the splendor
of his new sun porch, sipping wine
this fall evening, mosquitoes
in abeyance, fireflies rising
in a blaze of applause.

Where Will You Go When You Die?

Lord, with all due respect,
would it be OK if I just stayed here
in Cleveland, in my own backyard,
perhaps in the form of ashes
strewn in the flower garden?

I'll watch my kids playing in the sprinkler,
or chasing each other
with their lightsabers through summer.

I will observe my wife
grilling chicken on the barbecue,
not with the same skill, clearly,
as her late husband, although
she does seem to be improving,

as I can see from my vantage point
over here next to the hydrangeas,
which I so often failed to fertilize,
or weed, or even water
back when I was alive.

Make yourself useful,
she used to say, and here I am
doing exactly that.

Cheap Motels of My Youth

They lay somewhere between
the Sleeping In The Car era
and my current and probably final era,
the Best Western or Courtyard Marriott era.

The Wigwam. Log Cabin. Kozy Komfort
Hiway House. Star Lite. The Lazy A.

Just off the interstate, the roar
of the sixteen-wheelers all night long.
The dented tin door opening to the parking lot,
the broken coke machine muttering to itself.

"Color TV." "Free HBO." "Hang Yourself
in Our Spacious Closets." A job interview
at some lost-in-the-middle-of-nowhere
branch campus of some agricultural college
devoted to the research and development
of the soybean and related by-products.

Five-course teaching load, four of them
Remedial Comp. Candidate
must demonstrate familiarity
with the basic tenets of Christian faith.
Chance of getting the job
one in a hundred. Lip-sticked
cigarette butt under the bed.
Toilet seat with its paper band,
"Sanitized for Your Protection,"
dead roach floating in the bowl.

As the free HBO
flickers in the background,
you stare in the cracked mirror
at a face too young, too full of hope
to deserve this. And you wait
for the Courtyard Marriott era to arrive.

Dreamer

I spread my thumb and forefinger (my
father's thumb, grandfather's
forefinger) on the screen
to make a close-up, just a dark eye,
eyelid, eyebrow,
and show it to my wife.

That's me, she says, but I've fooled her.
It's our son's eye. Or

I haven't fooled her, it's her
eye, just spoken again, repeated,
retold, a new generation's
fresh articulation. Her
eye. But later,

when Michael
leans over his math, and draws
his shoulders up in frustration,
she says to me, that's
you. And she's right. There I am

for a flash, an instant, and there
is my grandfather, my great-
great-grandfather, leaning over
a table in Bitburg, Austria
by candlelight, cursing the numbers

in their rigid columns, their
unforgiving truth. He had never
been a practical man.

A dreamer, his mother said,
his wife said now. That's all
he was, all he would ever be.

Front Page

The family—the father and mother and two (cute) kids—
got into their private plane at the airport near the lake
and lifted off into the snowy night, into the weather,
and now here's this picture of the four of them
at Disneyland, and the picture is on the front page
of today's newspaper which is on our dining room table
where the four of us—father, mother, two (cute) kids—
are having pancakes on a late Sunday morning,
the snow falling outside, burying the deck chairs.
And I think of how it must have felt as the lake
came swimming up ravenously from the night
to devour them, the pale blue instruments
in the cockpit whirling, bleating in terror,
the father and mother working very hard
in the last clarifying seconds to formulate a phrase,
an utterance of sufficient magnitude,
a shouted finale involving love, that beautiful,
reliable old word that had rescued them
so many times before, and then
the impossible shock, the cold and darkness,
and now their photograph with the smiling mouse
on our battered dining room table
which my grandparents bought when they married,
my wife and I at the controls, steering this
ancient, well-built wooden craft through the snow,
the blinding snow that pushes at the windows,
while the kids dribble their syrup on the front page
and my wife is trying to be stern with them
but she can't stop laughing.

Daddy

Pallas Athena took my poetry course
one summer a few years back,
under some silly alias like Kristen
or Morgan, which didn't fool me
for a second. Full well I knew
that wide brow and gray eyes wherein
whole worlds revolved. As you know,
from time to time a god or goddess
hankers for a mortal, and so it was
that one day after class she waited
until the students had left the room,
then sat herself down on my desk,
Pallas Athena in tennis shorts
and a halter top with magical powers.
She asked me over to her place
for a Greek salad and blood-red
wine, Rioja, I think, although
everything was spinning, a roaring
from somewhere far off made it
impossible to hear. And I did pause,
I'll admit, for more than a few
blazing seconds as Troy burned,
I did hesitate before saying
no, sorry, my wife has lunch
waiting at home. Homer
gave an epic to his hero,
and a goddess or two as well.
My reward was a ham sandwich
and some iced tea. But when
I came home that day a small boy
wrapped his arms around my thigh
and cried out that strange name
whereby he knows me. Another
way of saying, *Odysseus*.

Avocados

My son comes into the kitchen
and asks if he can have an avocado.

A vo ca do, he says, loving the weight
of each green syllable on his tongue.

Avocados represent an immense step
for him, an evolutionary leap

far beyond the narrow confines
of cornflakes, wherein
he has dwelt for so long. The breast,
the cornflake, the avocado:
such has been his journey thus far.

You'll have to wait
until they're ripe, I tell him.
Want some cornflakes instead?
No thanks, he says, and wanders back
into the world of being five, while I—
I'm doing the dishes at this point—

I start thinking about ripening
and how glad I am that it takes time,

and his own ripening
will be years in the making. *Years*,
I say aloud, enjoying that long,
luxurious syllable, like a cat
stretching out on my tongue

as Michael comes in again,
it's been five minutes,
and asks, Are they ripe yet?

[…]

No, not quite yet.
Want some cornflakes in the meantime?

That's OK, he says. I'll wait.

Biker

I was due for a shower. So
I pulled up to a little motel,
the Wagon Wheel or some such,
in some dusty Nevada town,
and as I trudged across the parking lot
with my boots and bomber jacket,
my red bandana and scruffy beard,
the big old Harley cooling in the sun,
I saw, behind the office window,
a pale, slender arm reach down
and turn the Vacancy sign around
to No Vacancy.

O owner of the pale slender arm!
I have not forgotten you!
From thirty years down
that desert highway, from this life
of subcommittee meetings
and colonoscopies,
not to mention mortgage payments
and dental bills (braces
for *both* kids)—I'd just like to say
thank you—*thank you!*—for finding me
unkempt, and possibly smelly,
and for making me feel,
however briefly,
bad ass.

Misting

is the one thing involving flowers
I'm reasonably good at. Daybreak
finds me in the yard with my hose,
attentive as a bee. What a pleasure
to choose "Mist" on my watering gun
and drift like a cloud above the roses.
Last month my sister died, a storm
of lightning in her brain. And now
this news that someone who once
was the object of all my bouquets
is spending her final summer.
Each day brings more bad weather,
which is another way of saying
I'm in my sixties. But here, in the frail
September morning, my hand tipped in fog,
the flowers lift their faces to me
with bright, mystifying questions,
and for once I have an answer.

Multitasking

The pregnant young woman at the next table
is checking her phone while at the same time
crafting a delicate little skull, a couple of eyes,
and two beautifully sculpted ears,
not to mention a spleen and gall bladder.
She's finished the tiny trip-hammer
heart going lickety-split, so she texts
her mom while focusing quite intensely
on colon, rectum, etc., and the stomach
is just about wrapped up, but there's still
plenty of work to be done
on the spine, all those little bones,
and the central nervous system with its
confounding spaghetti of wiring,
and now she orders an espresso before
getting back to the toes, the feet, Jesus,
how many goddam bones does it take
to build somebody, but it's OK, no sweat,
she's actually enjoying it, and now
she texts her husband, *wine, Cheetos,
pickles*, OK, she shouldn't be drinking.
but it's just one glass at dinner,
and all I've done at my table is read
the obits, while she's already finishing up
the brain, which is always a challenge.

The Violations Man

appears one day on the sidewalk,
a nondescript individual
wearing a gray jacket and cap.
The violations man is holding a pen
and a clipboard, and he stands there
looking closely at my house, on which
I have made mortgage payments
for fifteen years. Mortgage
means "death pledge" in French,
as you may know. The violations man
stares at my house, nods his head
sadly, and writes something down.
Then something else. And something else.
Violations. I watch from the window.
There is nothing I can do.
Later, when I go outside
to walk to the local bakery
the violations man is still there.
He follows me down the sidewalk
with his clipboard and pen,
watching me, nodding sadly,
writing down violations.
When I get home with my bagels
he comes into the house with me.
My wife and I sit down at the table
with our bagels and coffee
and the violations man looks at us,
our kids, our life. He sighs
and nods his head sadly,
all the while writing down violations.
He is the violations man
and there is nothing we can do.

The St. Louis Trainyards

My wife sits on the sofa after dinner,
scrolling through some photos of the kids
playing on the sand in Mexico.
She is in the past, the wide beach of it,
the glittering, all-encompassing sea.
It is so easy to get there, so warm,
the ocean so inviting, no wonder
we go so often. I close my eyes
and join her there, the boys laughing
as they race each other into the waves.
And now I go back farther, it's just
so simple, back to my own father, not
at the seashore, but standing beside me,
his small boy, on a bridge high above
the St. Louis trainyards, great silver snarls
of track unwinding in the winter sun,
the boxcars booming far away, bending
toward the smoky horizon. We watch it all
dimly clanging beneath us, until
my father says it's time to go.

Insult to Injury

I find an old air gun
and a can of ammo
down in the basement
in a cardboard moving box,
along with some other stuff,
flotsam from previous lives.
A teenager, a long-expired
me, used it to polish off
tins cans in the backyard,
and once a bright, golden
oriole, shot in mid-song,
blowing a hole through me
as it fell. Holding a pistol
is like shaking hands
with death. What the hell,
let's see if the damn thing
still works. In the same box,
a volume of poetry, slim,
but not slim enough,
by a poet I never liked—
all smoke and mirrors—
a poet utterly, brutally
forgotten, although a blurb
on the back still calls his book
"an astonishing debut."
I prop it against the wall,
pump, load, cock, and *Blam*
goes the gun as it hasn't
in half-a-century. I inspect
the astonishing debut.
The pellet, as it happens,
made it farther than I ever did,
stopping on page sixty-two,

just deep enough to dimple,
not tear, a sonnet on the guy's
divorce, how his wife ran off
with his best friend, how terrible
the betrayal, how deep his grief.
How losing her tore out his soul.
And now this.

Minutes

That writer—the famous columnist
who got fired
for masturbating during a Zoom meeting—
I'm glad that happened. I mean,
I'm glad he got what was coming to him.

Because if we allow that sort of behavior
to go unchecked, among famous columnists
or just plain ordinary folks,

if people are masturbating on camera
instead of paying attention, taking notes
during important staff meetings,
meetings full of pressing issues
involving budgets, hiring policies,
curriculum planning, whatever—

if instead of attending to these issues,
everyone at the important Zoom meeting
just sits there masturbating—well,
that meeting won't be very productive, will it?

And the minutes—the minutes
would be ridiculous.

Being Helpful

I was maybe twelve and my mother
came home from grocery shopping.
It was a hot day in mid-summer
and as I lifted a bag from the trunk
the bottom ripped and a bottle
of red wine fell and shattered
on the driveway, the wine bleeding
into the asphalt and my mother
looked down and burst into tears
for the little dirt farm she grew up on
in Illinois, for my father dead
of Scotch, for the pistol her brother
put to his head, for everything lost
and for the crummy little house
in a sunbaked California subdivision,
for the double shifts at the nursing home,
the Olds leaking oil, for everything
she could never give us, for the night
ahead of her in front of the TV,
sit coms and Carson, stone cold sober.

Archaic Poet Listens to Bach

after Rilke

On my morning walk to the train station
I hear a violinist practicing, the notes
falling from a window three floors up,
floating onto the trees, enchanting
the hedges and flowerbeds, because
the violinist is good. Very good.
It's Bach's *Chaconne, Partita Number 2,*
both excruciatingly beautiful
and fiendishly difficult to play,
and as I stand there, enraptured,
I realize that never in my life
have I achieved such mastery, never
have I risen to a challenge so great.
And I make a solemn vow to myself
right then and there: You must change
your morning route to the train station.

Rock Shop

Our kids look at the rocks
in their little boxes,
the names hand-printed
on index cards—pyrite,
amethyst, onyx, calcite—
assessing color, weight,
or just some mysterious
rock essence they are young
and primal enough to feel,
and since the rocks are only
a dollar, we say yes,
and the rocks are taken home
and placed on bookshelves
and immediately forgotten,
which is understandable.

So the rocks just sit quietly,
gathering dust, plodding
through time at rock speed,
as our kids blaze through time
at kid speed in the backyard,
and my wife cooks lasagna
while I mow the lawn,
and in one million or ten
million years the rocks are still
sitting there and we are
the dust covering them,
which is not understandable.

Empty Chair Problem

A bunch of old men meet
at the café every morning.
The ROMEOS, they call themselves.
Retired Old Men Eating Out.
They sit there and chew over
the present and the past,
they pore over the mystery
of what brought them here
to this final redoubt, they have
some decaf and maybe a bagel.
Now and then—every year or so—
one of them doesn't show up,
for the simple reason
that he has ceased to be.
He is no longer here
where the rest of us are
and for a few weeks the group
leaves his chair vacant
and his "no longer hereness"
throbs and pulses from that chair
like a living thing until one day
the chair is occupied by a new
old guy, and what I'd like to suggest,
obvious as it may be, is that
whatever makes these guys
"not here" always seems to come
when they're away from the table,
so why not consider just staying
at the table permanently?
Keep your guard up, post
a lookout, take turns sleeping,
and by no means turn off the lights.
Give it a try, and maybe, just maybe,
we can solve this "empty chair problem."

Abandoned Bicycle

A bicycle—a nice one—
has been locked to the lamp post
all summer and fall.

Tires gone flat.
A congregation of leaves
worshipping the wheels.

And on the brake levers
and the tiny bolts
that held the seat exactly
where someone wanted it to be,
rust is constructing
its sprawling embassies.

Maybe a drunk drifted
over yellow lines. A clot
formed in the thigh
and moved north.
Or somebody just got
sick and tired.

Anyway, the bike is waiting.
Its metals gleam urgently.

Soon the scavengers will come.
The pedals—unable to live
without each other—will vanish
into a fresh new marriage.

The seat will disappear
into a seat-shaped abyss.

[...]

One night, someone
will help himself to a wheel.
Not quite a bicycle,
but a start.

And the bike,
like an abandoned person,
will become a clock,
calibrated to measure
the precise duration
of loneliness.

Across the Field

On the third-floor balcony
of the apartment building
across the weedy lot from us,
a woman wheels her daughter out
each evening to watch the sun set.

She is gray-haired, slow-moving.
The daughter is perhaps thirty.
They smoke contentedly, they sip
their wine as the summer dusk
gutters and burns down,
and from across the field
I can hear, not the words,
but the music of their talk.

I can't pretend to know
what the mother feels about this,
how the daughter lives in her chair.
But as I listen
to their laughter, as the day
dwindles and their cigarettes
flare like stars, it looks
as if happiness can start
a small fire anywhere.

Salad

It is a summer evening
in 1948. My mother and father
are in the backyard
of the little duplex they rented.
Summer evening
in St. Louis. I have yet
to exist but nonetheless
I know that two hamburgers
are on the grill, and the beer
is cold in the humid dusk.
A dog barks next door,
my father turns the burgers,
my mother goes in
to set the table for two
and make a salad. There's
more beer in the fridge.
They don't even have a TV.
Nobody does. In the kitchen
that does not include me
the burgers are great,
and my father says something
that makes my mother laugh
so hard that I can hear her
in my backyard tonight
in Cleveland, where thanks
to them I exist
at the grill, a beer
in my hand, a dog barking,
my wife in the kitchen
making a salad.

ABOUT THE RATTLE CHAPBOOK SERIES

The Rattle Chapbook Series publishes and distributes a chapbook to all of *Rattle*'s print subscribers along with each quarterly issue of the magazine. Most selections are made through the annual Rattle Chapbook Prize competition (deadline: January 15th). For more information, and to order other chapbooks from the series, visit our website.

THE SMILE OF THE ACROBAT
England, Tallahassee, Europe

AUDREY WILSON

Prospect Press
Sistersville, WV
New York, NY

Grateful acknowledgment is made to the following publications in which some of these poems have appeared:

FSPCA *Anthology Fourteen* "Olympic Gymnasts."

Apalachee Quarterly "Opera Afternoons."

Legend "Purple Iris" and "Schubert's Death and the Maiden Quartet"

Penumbra "Fuzzy Logic in a Mozart Allegro," "Klee Watercolor: Colorful Life Outside," and "Lepers' Squint."

Poetry Now (U.K.) "That Time of Year" and "*Wallflowers in England."

Sparrowgrass Poetry Forum "Schubert," "Insomnia," "By Chance," and "Rilke."

Published by Prospect Press
609 Main Street
Sistersville, West Virginia 26175

Library of Congress Catalog Card Number: 99-076296

ISBN: 1-892668-20-3

Manufactured in the United States of America

First Edition

10 9 8 7 6 5 4 3 2 1

that smile . . . .
Angel! Oh, take it, pluck it, that small-flowered herb of healing!

Shape a vase to preserve it . . . .
praise it, with florally soaring inscription:
"Subrisio Saltat." (The Smile of the Acrobat)

Translated from Rilke's "Fifth Elegy" celebrating Picasso's "Les Saltimbanques" by J.E. Leishman and Stephen Spender, London: Hogarth Press, 1948, 59.

For my sister

Keith, Mark, Erwin and Edwin, pillars of support,

with especial thanks to Mark, a friend's friend,
for his insight, criticism and encouragement

and to Debby, point of perspective.

TABLE OF CONTENTS

ENGLAND

TALLAHASSEE

ENGLAND

EUROPE

TALLAHASSEE

ENGLAND

*WALLFLOWERS IN ENGLAND

Virgilian velvet
lies within
these flowers

Imperial red and Dido's gold
maroon the deaths of kings
with lavender for rue
the faded rose of columbine
and chestnut glossy brown
the yellow of the sun
all drowsing in their honeyed haze

And after boring years in school
of Caesar's Gallic Wars
on May the third began
the glorious *Aeneid*

A window was ajar
and from the flowered wall
rolled wave on fragrant wave
which Virgil adumbrated
until the velvet petals were
transmuted into Latin

*Four petalled fragrant flowers of many colors. It is believed that their
seeds were in the stone the Normans brought to England in 1066
(Botanical Gardens, Cambridge).

ENGLAND

LEPERS' SQUINT

Go back six centuries
to Ticehurst village church.
There still were lepers then
who lived outside in fields
or in deserted fields.
Perhaps the people left out food,
they must have done
for how could lepers work
with toes and fingers gone?
This Christian charity was cheap
compared to kindly touch,
contagion feared by all.

Outside the church the ground
was high towards the east
and here they cut the squint,
a square carved in the wall
that slid into a slit
above the altar and the Host.
When summoned by church bell
and all the rest were safe inside
through here the living dead
could see the wine and see the bread
that brought Communion.

ENGLAND

THAT TIME OF YEAR

From empty boughs in winter woods
the Gothic vault arose,
the stone as intricate
as interwoven stems,
both laced with light
from sky or window stain.
The masons also knew
how if a stone were thrown
into a pool
the ripples were far flung
then crossed in measured steps.
They swung those dancing circles up
into the stone
and threaded them through boughs
so wood and pool were there
with glancing light askance
to make the Gothic vault.

Did Shakespeare mean by ruined choirs
where monks were used to sing
or only birds?

BLUE HYDRANGEAS

Rilke said hydrangeas
did not hold their blue
but reflected it from far
wishing it were lost,
blue of ancient stationery,
yellow, violet and grey.

These hydrangeas are the blue
quattrocento painters knew,
Mary's robes were of this hue,
in the woods the bluebells too
singing alleluia.

ENGLAND

AIR RAID SHELTER

The sound of fear is loud loud loud,
"Our guns, not bombs," they say;
the sound is just the same
except at first when bombers come
there is a low insistent drumming
that grinds along the spine,
with bombs exploding very near
each brings a curdling whine
but otherwise the noise the same,
the sound of fear is loud loud loud.

Spring falls across the mountains now
in musical delight
with swallow wings through evening air
and summer's silken light
is caught within its flight.
What use is that just now?

The sound of fear is loud loud loud
and death so near
and life so near
and both unknown;
with hands lost in hair
becoming aware
fragility of hands,
the sound of fear is loud loud loud.

Be still and feel the silence
three hundred miles away
as death roars through the drunken sky
and night aches for the day,
through all the tortured hours hear
the clear transparent springs
that echo down the shadowed hills
and in abandon stream away
and so perfection find.
Spring falls across the mountains now
but only in the mind.

ENGLAND

AFTER A RAID

Like tulips spring the workmen's fires
on mornings carved in snow
and faces lost in dark iced air
to life leap in the glow

The year is bound in bitter chains
the power of night supreme
the tender light of flowering fires
is waking from a dream

and how they hurt the sombre air
like early daffodils
that rising ache to meet the light
that often chills or kills

We hold such walls before the air
afraid to feel or sing
but flowers and fires give all away
and a child could die on a swing.

ENGLAND

DUNKIRK MEMORY

Halycon days—unusual phrase
meaning calm at sea—
heard on radio.
Voice announcing
"Army stranded at Dunkirk
bombed and shelled
Navy ships inadequate
to evacuate
most in use elsewhere;
England now needs every craft
motor rowboat sail canoe
halycon days the seas are calm
cross the Channel now today
bring our army home."

Channel death to all small craft
waves could overwhelm
halycon days the water smooth
Channel full of little boats
Air Force kept off German planes
some broke through
many boats were lost
most returned again again
army saved by little boats
never known in history.

Decades later paddleboat
showing tourists River Thames
bore the plaque
Dunkirk 1940
deeds of valor done that day
Dunkirk stands with Agincourt.

ENGLAND

MUSIC IN WARTIME   London was bombed for nine months, 1940-
1941, and during the time Myra Hess organized lunchtime concerts at the
National Gallery. The paintings had been moved to a cave in North
Wales; Churchill said: "Let them be buried in the bowels of the earth but
not one painting leaves this island." One painting was left: Botticelli's
Mars and Venus. No one know why that painting remained but it was
obvious that Venus triumphed.

LUNCHTIME CONCERT

The clock outside strikes two
but at the chime
the bow across the violin
has cancelled time.
There is apart from time
no ugliness;
though heavy squat the man
yet as he leans across the strings
he draws a tender curve.

ST. JOHN PASSION: BACH

The waters of the music
have washed into the mind
whose pendulum held still attends
the falling of a wave,
another voice to sound.

The wave hangs in the air
and she the singer waits
as in the Middle Ages
a listening angel leant,
entranced in waiting
poised above
the chasms of the chords.

PURPLE IRIS

Purple is dark with the deaths of kings
and purple the iris stand.
The shabby room is cold
flaunting in arrogance they flame
seizing as proud medieval tyrants
from conquered surrounding subjects
power life and gold.
The room fades to the curved petals
slowly revealing their light.

Their darkness is bright with splendor
deathly dark they shine in the gloom
and penetrate even the silence
to the sound of a viol d'amor.

ENGLAND

7 A.M. BUS PORTMADOC

How liquid the chimneys in the morning
as birds pour through the dawn
in glinting slits of sunlight
their icy chill cascades.

A darkened door   firelit within
a red-haired child runs down the street
a morning street of shadows
where even stones are long and thin
her hair first flame then copper leaves.

The village ends   the road goes on
through javelins of yellow gorse
to splendor of the tawny hills
a lion's crouching paws.

BANGOR

Beyond the streets the dandelions
strode fiercely to the sea
but still the town was in the clouds
and smoke from many chimneys rose
slow fountains that would never fall
and gulls wove through these scattered strands
their wild embroidery.
With clouds for sails and rigged with smoke
and decks of dandelions
the town sailed on the sea.

NORTH WALES

BUSINESS GIRL

His memo of the eighteenth June—
what did it say, where is it now?
The heavens fall and earth stands still
for it is lost no matter how.

Perhaps it slyly came attached
on to a clip and so crept in
a file where it did not belong
and thus the world hangs on a pin.

But to remember what it said,
what it did not, or did imply.
did he say yes, or was it no,
if so, to whom and how and why?

O memory be kind swoop down
and bring this note to life again
but don't bring other memories
to muddle a distracted brain.

No use to think of strange square bones,
the shining black of grazing cow,
with purple foxgloves round her flank,
no use at all just now.

No use to look out and enjoy
the sun aslant across the wall,
the dusty honey colored stone
so warm and old—no use at all.

And why reflect that though his face
now looks as if it were of wood,
if hung upon a bare white wall
his death mask doubtless would be good?

But what is this, o wild delight,
o ecstacy beyond compare!
"You mentioned the meeting of thirteenth June
and stated that you were not there."

NORTH WALES

SEASIDE PARLOR

The piano stands erect and staid
unloved for nothing lingers
above its white indifferent keys
no echoes of thin melodies
for nothing stirred its barren soul
except perhaps a Barcarolle
made simple for the unskilled fingers
of those who won certificates
for swimming   diving and first aid
certificates with ancient dates
that long adorned the flowered walls
and now unnoticed fade.

Two pots of hideous design
obstruct the view and draw the eye
as pavement pictures sometimes hold
those waiting to pass by.
A massive clock ornate and black
that never went since Father died
has lions and leaves embossed on top
and horses rearing at each side.
The gently falling sunlit dust
can find no resting place
but through the mirror sweep the gulls
on wings of grace.

NORTH WALES

EARLY MORNING TRAIN

In morning trains the grimy windows
are smeared with dust that turns to steam
the heavy faces are lined masks
and putty grey they seem.

Dull water trickles down the panes
but when the winter sun appears
seen through a thousand thin cascades
of slowly falling tears
these change to shining palaces
of sunlit ice and air
high arched like vast cathedrals
of liquid gossamer.

And through these airy vaulted spires
a strange land rolls away
enscrolled in smoke and torn with fog
and pierced by shafts of day.
A sudden stretch of water gleams
and swans whose wings are clouds of light
glide through receding veils of mist
last curtains of the night.

HARDLY A SONNET

Was it so hard to watch a stream
to wait awhile and simply stare
adrift in some consoling dream
you hurried by and left it there
the truth impossible to bear.
So many things have you betrayed
with longing for an unknown love
so as to dull the tearing knife
of beauty as it struck your life
and would have set you free
had you but dared to stand alone
alone had dared to see
beyond the veils of loneliness
perfection in a tree

ENGLAND

THE DEAD ARE NOW WITHIN

The dead are now within
because they smiled in such a way
so now we smile today
and what they felt so still we feel
the dead are now within.

A time worn glass   a half lit room
a strange face   not her own
a strange face floated on the gloom
and she stepped back and watched it drown
away among the shadows.

Soft heavy silks were in her hands
and in her ears a minuet
the high arched room familiar too
ten pointed windows open wide
with mirrors in between.
The night was dark outside
but stealing in among the silks
then lost around the chandeliers
where shadow moths danced to their deaths
through candle constellations.
The candles burned from sunlit wine
reflected dimmed in polished wood
pale swans on midnight pools.
The candles slid through mirrors
down arms as satin smooth as nuts
alight with jewels
and in her dress   its paniered folds
rose colored peaches in the mist
as heavy soft to touch.
The dresses swept as wind sweeps leaves
around   around   around
as slow as autumn falls
and through it all the violins
as spears of thin delight
one moment long
forever.

Her face stared back afraid
the dead are now within.

ENGLAND

13

THE CRYPT

The night was swift outside
it raced the moonlight past the car
and shadows chased along beside
besieging all the windows
across   across her hands they fell
and in her hands she held
a flower of the moon
magnolia.
There every petal was an arch
and when the shadows moved
the silent curves were changed
and these she wandered through
as in a crypt
so cool within her hands
and cool within her mind
the flowering of the stone.

ENGLAND

AUTUMN BEE

With rigging threaded in the clouds
the shabby boats lolled on the sea
which drained their faded paint away
until like floating seeds they lay,
the winged seeds of sycamores.

A buoy jubilant in red
was in the pulsing stream
while gulls moved through the afternoon
along each other's bones.
The hills slept on   the shadows grew
the clouds slid deeper in the sea
as they into their dream.
A bumble bee fell in the boat
a dying autumn bee
with summer still on languid wings
they rowed it back to shore
nastursiums were its pyre.

ENGLAND

BITTER FRUIT
Set to music by Howard Wilson

Oh you who stand awhile amazed
beneath the hush of snow
that falling slides through cherry boughs
in sunlit silence slow,
shake not the branches' winged foam
upon her shining hair
believing love the swansdown light
that floats upon the air
for in her eyes sleep memories
of bruised forgotten years
with all the scars of olden wars
a thousand buried fears.
Beneath this drifting blossom trails
a tangled winding root
and from these snowlit boughs will blow
a darkly bitter fruit.

ENGLAND

ROSE

A dark rose filled with rain
light is not wrapped within
it is the blood beneath the skin
a petal curves and light pours forth.

Let it lie upon a page
whose purity and thin dark letters seem
the only things are not shamed.
The room shrinks back
the soft round petal on the copper leaf
a naked shoulder leans
against a smooth insentient door.
Let darkness fall around this rose
deep among the shadows gleams the rain
the shadows on grapes   the shadows in flames
the images are shadows

Be silent now and see
the rose lies by a poem
a marriage then is born
the air alive with wings
one breath
be silent   do not think
the rose lies on the page
as if awaiting love
and in its full surrender
there is the whole of love.

All this is dust and nothing worth
the rose is the reality
no death
within this dream

ENGLAND

17

TRAIN STATION

Waiting in a station and the train is late.
The minutes stretch their seconds out
until it seems that they will snap
like glass spun in the fire too long
and still it does not come.
The crashing brakes of other trains
beat with the blood along the veins
into the heart   into the brains
and still it does not come.

The sun pours through the slatted roof
in railroad tracks thin tracks of light
that cleave the dust and rising smoke
and intersect the shadows
and iron and mist and stone and steam
are fading phantoms of a dream
to one who wakes reluctantly
to harsh reality
the train is the reality
the train that never comes.

ENGLAND

TAPESTRY

In other days how plunging grief
was woven into tapestry
in slanted threads repeatedly
devouring inches fashioning
a tilted petal   bending leaf
of faded rose or flickering green
and all the shades of in between
to crush the endless hours down
of patience wearing at the bone
to stitches pricking life away
in yet another row

WINTER AFTERNOON

A winter afternoon
the water silk a swan sails through
as in a mirror drowned.
The light is shaken to see
the golden trees and their long shadows
it could be summer from the shadows
for all the hills are warm
but berries prick into the air
sharp against the floating hair
of tangled stems and thorns
and silver birches stand afraid
of winter who will capture them.
They need not fear for their white skin
his touch on them is light.

ENGLAND

PAIN

Night broke through her daytime mask
flung the gates of pain
open wide, the weight of worlds
held her once again.

Thunder without glory roared
crashing jaws of steel
giant machines announced the doom—
all who dared to feel.

Books and painting turned away
leaving her distress
knowing that she could not bear
silent tenderness.

From a grey stone ginger jar
leaping flames sprang to the light,
dahlias born of wine and fire
burning through the night.

One flared high to reach the lamp
laughed exulting in its power
so she laid her weariness
on this daring flower.

Then it gently held her pain
everything receded far
the cloth with holes the coffee stain
even the grey jar.

World a dahlia without care
cloud on fire in evening sky,
morning found it smouldering
                first to die.

ENGLAND

20

THE WINTER JOURNEY
Schubert

The earth is kind to those in pain
the grass slides shadow cool
though bruised yields only gentleness
to the distracted fool
who clings to it to find release
and thin grass sighing fills the air
to echo on the wild despair
despair will never cease
for when one heart is quiet again
still blinded children wake afraid
and people die unloved alone
there is no end to pain.

There is no end to all the wounds
inflicted fresh each day
but only single footsteps sound
on Schubert's icy way
for there in flowering loveliness
still shines the linden tree,
transparent leaves are frozen tears
a falling melody
which shakes the heart in vain
for he found no returning road
there is no end to pain.

Yet in the fierce touch of the earth
lies tenderness that calms
and bones give up their agony
in everlasting arms.

ENGLAND

SONNET SEQUENCE
Second sonnet set to music by Howard Wilson

If consolation lies in words that rhyme
its source is hidden well as though the stream
ran under rocks that stood as dark as time
against all search   defenders of the dream.
The dream the words defend was once a power
that burst the chains that bound it in the brain
of someone now it waits until the hour
imagination wakens it again.
As chimney smoke all through a summer's day
hangs still unmoved suspended in the light
and no winds blow to scatter it away
so still and poised must one be who would find
the dream   then deep the chimes fall through the night
the vision falls into the silent mind.

The vision falls into the silent mind
and thoughts that clutched like closely tangled trees
with all their knotted branches thick entwined
are now so still   as calm as morning seas
that slide out of the hills at dawn and wait
until the glory shall in peace descend.
The vision falls and glory without end
streams down at last as terrible as fate
but first the load that manacled the brain
as heavy as the world   this load of thought
must be removed   a Herculean strain
for thoughts are wild with life and anguished fight
against the peace at length so dearly bought
their death alone releases wings of light.

SCHUBERT'S "DEATH AND THE MAIDEN" QUARTET

Against the peace at length so dearly bought
she struggled   pushing back the dread unknown
and Schubert knew how bitterly she fought
to find a love whose beauty would atone
for everything she had to lose. Her life
was longing filled with fierce desire
to penetrate the darkness as a fire
her only fear an ending of that strife
that waged between her and the outer world
its wonder and its pain. She had to stay
to know the answer   step by step she hurled
defiance until all had gone but pride.
as death tore that last shield away
love came to her at last as to a bride.

ENGLAND

PREGNANCY

This child shall know of England,
around the lake around around
each footfall pressing pregnancy
into the ground
three times clockwise around.

An exile far away
this holiday a lane
led to the lake where nightingales
were used to sing in short May nights
in sprays of sound
a bubbling up a splashing down
to Keats and white hawthorn.
That day they did not sing
but still in memory
around the lake around around
each footfall pressing pregnancy
into the ground
three times clockwise around.

And after twenty years
her son and she returned.
He knew the Kentish Weald
where through the night the church bells sound.
They stopped the further end of lake
and did not walk from left to right
which troubled her. Full circle round,
he said.

ENGLAND

TALLAHASSEE

OPERA AFTERNOONS

For years the snake and I
lay on the ground but separate
divided by the leaves;
the sun was his attraction
while I preferred the shade.
The boughs swayed to the music,
perhaps he heard it too.
Erratic squirrels launched
their flights above us both,
disturbing patterned shade
but only for a while
until the time of day.
The garden was not theirs
and it did not belong
to the dividers of the air,
that bringing sharp delight
remained among the leaves.

Possession is of the ground;
it was the snake's and mine.
He died on Easter Saturday,
I thought it was his skin
and he would be renewed,
but at *The Meistersingers* end
I saw it was his death.

TALLAHASSEE

FLORIDA MORNING

Blue shadows guard the grass
from tiger sun
attack;
recalling English light
dew-heralded through grass
arousing the roses
to flutes or oboes
with dazzle of scent,
but here the sudden juice
a hard green apple spurts
approximates.

AFTER A DROUGHT

Green is for all the delight,
rain with its sounding fulfillment
sliding the sharp cooling shafts
slanting the flowers and trees
slashing them into the dance
wave upon echoing wave
slicing aquarium air,
deep is the well of delight.

Green were the mountains once
young in the morning
lifting a slumbering sea,
greener the pools at evening
under the flickering wings,
dark stood the reeds, darker the bats
splintering watery gloom,
deeper the well of delight.

TALLAHASSEE

FUZZY LOGIC IN A MOZART ALLEGRO

As in a bubble chamber
the fractured light explodes
cascading down
as in a stream
the glitter
shifts several depths
of space
the mind entranced
awaits
another note to soar
parabola of sound
shattering the shadow
of a quark.

TALLAHASSEE

NEUTRINOS

Looking at darkness
what do eyes see?
Spider webs scintillating
endlessly agitating
ceaseless activity
dusk has no peace.
Atoms are sizzling
drizzling
fizzling
with neutrinos that back into time
chaos is churning the night

PHILOSOPHY

"The drag behind the edge
of actuality"
                said Dr. Ice.
Behind the present moment peers
with clutching hands yet manacled
a crowd in jostling tiers
the shadows of the past.
They strive to grasp the thin edged knife
to touch the moment cut in time
and disappear
appealing for remembrance
and in their interrupted cries
the whisper of the future sounds
potentiality.

TALLAHASSEE

SCHROEDINGEN FROM A HUMANIST POINT OF VIEW

Electrodes are but standing waves
or nodes between the waves
as when in skipping rope
the length and height are seen
or when a stone is thrown
into a pool
addition of dimension depth;
this can be seen or visualized
but only true of hydrogen.

In other atoms electrons
have standing waves
of multiple dimension
of probability
and this requires a leap
beyond imagination
and yet discoveries are made
upon this supposition
and proven to be true
by modern physicists.

A faith in God cannot be proved
and yet results are seen:
does modern physics differ
from a belief in God?

TALLAHASSEE

MY SONS

JOHN

A little boy asleep,
the wind saws his gold cloud hair
and frets his nectarine cheek,
relaxed he droops
a fruit so fair
whose beauty will not keep.

ANDREW

Child who was you throw the ball
cut off by the years.
From a photo your eyes startle,
a forgotten grace,
ball, thin arm and serious face
irrecoverably lost,
lacrimae rerum.*

*Virgil, *Aeneid*, Book I, line 655, is usually translated in English as "the
tears of things."

KEITH

Enigma
vaulting thought
you need no spur
save inwit
you know the end
before the end
aware of more than knowledge
so now you leap
and how who knows
beyond the centuries
"The white rose of York."

TALLAHASSEE

SIN

There was a lecturer
who could teach Chaucer well
the Wife of Bath
the Franklyn's Tale
the Miller's too
beyond all that
concept of courtesye.
She then grew old
retired and was alone.
She phoned me once to visit her
but I was teacher then
with children
and the harassment.
"Three baseball games this week
a birthday party too
and finals to correct,
I cannot come," I said
and this was sin
if there be sin
as Karma holds
for which I should be held
responsible
for which I claim
redemption.
"This aye nighte, this aye nighte,
everye nighte and alle,
fire and sleete and candlelighte
and Christe receive my soule."

For Dr. Herndon

TALLAHASSEE

RAINED OUT BALL GAME

In pouring rain men still
continue pouring sand on mud
and will not cancel game

Madonna face with gum
eyes rolling at each chew
her ash blond hair pulled back
a van der Weyden look
exquisite line of jaw
distorted by the gum
turns into a van Bosch:
a bulbous monster leaps
between her lips and sprawls
across her face
in writhing coils of pink
the entrails of a pig
the viscera perhaps
and no one notices
accustomed to obscenities.

In pouring rain men still
continue pouring sand on mud
and will not cancel game

TALLAHASSEE

M.A.L.

Among Elysian fields
where Schubert's stream descends
one day I shall be watching
thin grasses hold the rain
or how a birch bark etches
a Leonardo stain
a whistle then will sound
the leaves will hold their trees.
Before the blessed spirits
can echo from afar
I shall have the pleasure
of knowing who you are.

THE HUNTER

Earth and air
ancient humours
inextricably entwined
in creativity.
The hunter very much of earth
awaits the squirrel's leap
the tension of the haunch,
primordial bond between
the killer and the killed
in paleolithic walls
experienced in thought.

TALLAHASSEE

JENNIFER

Stay forever child
contemplating music
how to move your thoughts
in dance
whether wing cartwheel or horse
whether girl you soon will be
curve of waltz
insouciance
into
somersault

TALLAHASSEE

DAYLIGHT SAVING

Turn back the clock
another summer gone
and time unnoticed long
among his sliding leaves
stands sentinel again.

Accompanied by bells
each hour used to strike his tread
through crowded day in darkened night
but clocks no longer tick
when minutes fall away
and digits do not trace his path
as dials used to do
yet twice a year
at spring and fall
when tampering with time
his presence felt.

SENSE OF TIME

Carriage clock at night
hanging in the dark
letting moments slide
under horses' hooves
pressed before the half
chimed the previous hour
after half the next
casual sense of time
give or take an hour

but now
clutching at each second
when the light turns red
grabbing on the wheel
gnashing of the teeth
as the moments pass
when the traffic stalls
lost the nonchalance
of the carriage clock

TALLAHASSEE

CROSSING THE ATLANTIC

Another world than this
with ships instead of wings
and after many days
of watching empty seas
with longing for the further shore
at last a long low line of white;
this time no breaking edge of foam
nor far away the wings of gulls
perhaps at first a memory
but then in morning light
the chalk white cliffs of home.

TALLAHASSEE

ENGLAND

AND AFTER MANY YEARS

And after many years
the pale green fields and charcoal trees
with glints of silver where the willow
has caught the pallid light.
Afar among the trees
a house blooms
a petal of the sky   a pearl
re-echoed in the puddles
that glitter the hillside.
Four poplars stand   a pleasure
and like the crocus blades
as bold and cold as birds.

A primrose caught in light
is unforgettable
forever in the mind
but seen again
champagne.

ENGLAND

TALLAHASSEE FROM ENGLAND

A blue jay calls and two far worlds connect.
Beneath unclouded skies
azaleas froth like butterflies
camelias carved in wax
the olive petalled dogwood flower
the green gold chalice with the broken edge
there ripens lightens whitens
into morning snow.

In England fickle clouds
allow the rain like pearls
to filter down through silk
then melt upon the land as light
and roll away above a field
to lift one corner up
and slip the rest in shade.

Light blazons into daffodils
as lanterns for a child;
a primrose holds a drop of light
but cools the hand.
The trees hold empty boughs
but light is caught within
through buds that warm the air,
like antique cups of crazed glass
alight with wine they stand.
The clouds have spilt their shadows down
like woods across the fields
the real woods are umber
the woods of cloud are blue
Titian blue.

The jay still calls and this is where
the roots are laid
entangled in the light and shade
of this cloud shadow land.

ENGLAND

VARIATIONS ON OLD THEMES

The flowers under candlelight
have caught
eternity.
So far beyond the world
their enchanted spirits sail
that to the eyes of angels
their petals are unfurled.

The wealth of chestnut trees in bloom
the chandeliers of flowers wind
through green and glorious gloom
to splinter light among the leaves
and overwhelm the mind.

The seas of bluebells wave on wave
pour over the hillside.
The scent of hyacinth
subdues the sense.
Was it from this the painters chose
the blue of the Madonna's robes
to show their adoration?

ENGLAND

KNOLE PARK

Elizabeth the First
gave to the Sackville-Wests
for service to the crown
a noble manor house.
The rooms rolled on forever
fourposter beds for kings and queens
or dukes and duchesses
with tapestries still hanging
to keep away the cold
for damask lasts for centuries.

A bare and simple room
with single couch and bolster* there
where in the sixteenth century
a maiden lady lived
of whom no one knew much
an aunt of someone long since dead;
infirmity prevented her
from eating in the hall
her meals were brought on trays
she lived her life alone
and held the bolster all the time.

As when all feeling gone
and memory withdrawn
a voice can raise a tone
that shivers down the spine
this tale returns.

*bolster—a long thin pillow.

ENGLAND

LONDON GARDENS

Along the London Rail
the gardens twelve foot square
with sweet pea rose and hollyhock
are deeds of valor which arise
from deep within the genes
to resurrect
the flowers falling everywhere
through scented light and shade
in meadow lane or cottage gate
in gardens long ago
and now in city spread
these bright enamelled squares
are daring revelations
of loss and need.

NORTH WALES

STONE WALLS IN WALES

Sheep, pearls stitched
among the hills,
another tone of stone,
clover, clouds another;
the walls
pearl silver ebony and rust
stone on stone
as slow as sheep
across the hills
or clouds
or centuries.

NORTH WALES

EUROPE

KLEE WATERCOLOR:
Colorful Life Outside

May evenings were light and long
for one who "liked so much to play
but had to go to bed by day. . . ."
so RLS* an age ago
and now again today.
The children in thin zigzag blue
are floating by along the light
as frail and winged squares,
their echoes sound beyond the day
in counterpointed space.
The bell weaves time.

*Robert Louis Stevenson

Chur, SWITZERLAND

SOGLIO

They used to call it Badedas
but now it's Vita Bath Spring Green
a bubble path of chestnut woods.
In Soglio in snow
the huts of chestnuts climb
the mountain woods
for men have known for centuries
that chestnut oil was balm for bones.
A count once owned the land
and built a splendid house and left
but others climbed the winding ways
and made the healing oil.
For months the chestnuts dry on boards
beneath the roofs against the snow
sun rain and moon
until the time is ripe for oil
a patient trade.

The poet Rilke stayed a while,
the narrow steps and wrought iron grilles
reminded him of childhood Prague.
While there he wrote "Primeval Sound"
and sent it to the artist Klee
who recreated it in paint
through winding ways.

Soglio, SWITZERLAND

HAIKU FROM SWITZERLAND

Javelins of snow
push through cloud to reach last light
eluding white sails

blackbird evening spills
liquid bars of bronze and dark
from recumbent hills

beech in leaf above
last year's rust below   cowbells announce
melting fields of snow

Iseltwald and Muerten, SWITZERLAND

FROM PIAZZA MICHELANGELO

The green cool river glides between
exquisite mansions drowned within;
their shuttered windows steeply stained
and gold facades refracting light
from here and there
throughout late afternoon
till night subdues the river
to green translucency
which hangs suspended there
between the bridges thread on air
and spun with lamps that echo far
into the hills and then come home
where white and bronze the tulip burns
of Brunelesschi's dome.

FLORENTINE WINTER

Thin silver spears of olive leaves
beyond the heavy wall
spur on the weary footsteps
ascending the steep hill
to Belvedere Fort.

A sudden turn reveals
the city down below
ablaze in afternoon
the Duomo a flame
with windows jewelled in palaces
by slanting shafts of sun
while far above upon the height
dark cypresses in golden light
no longer can hold back the night
from rolling down the hill.

Florence, ITALY

NIGHTINGALES IN PROVENCE

They sang because they had to sing,
a bubbling up, a splashing down
a murmuring on
unceasingly,
and with the long awaited note
the ancient poets rang
their bells along the night
till darkness smiled again.

CHERRIES IN PROVENCE

Round shapes of pearl and sudden red
drop down from pointed leaves
dark angles on the globes
enhance the light
refracted from the fruit
alive as water drops
or oboes
chromatic notes that fall and fall
sustained within the scale.

Provence, FRANCE

LA BAGATELLE ROSE GARDEN

The roses are confined
by geometric hedge
and wooden trellis squares
as though Platonic form
were needed to invoke
the quintessential rose.

From white to ivory
from light of palest moon
to wax more golden with each flower
to alpine afterglow
rose petals crushed with Chardonnay
and then with Beaujolais
from apricot to nectarine
then flushed with Burgundy become
a damson or a plum
till every scent and taste and shade
was spiritually transformed
into another world
where all the senses one.

PARIS

RILKE
Caroussel, Jardin des Plantes

Dead poet who loved Paris
your faded caroussel
of panthers, bears, giraffes
still rearing up
and circling round
the music grinding on

no elephant is there
not even now and then
so magical for you
a century ago
the music grinding on

no children riding now
but did they just dismount
or was it years long since
they disappeared from view
the music grinding on?

PARIS

SCHUBERT

Child in the mountains at night,
fireflies were piercing the fields
sprinkling the scent of the hay
grasses occasionally lit.
Someone was singing there down by the lake
lamps were reflected in drops
music was seizing the dark
"Schubert" suggested a voice
no one remembered the song,
always remaining unknown
sweeter than anything else.
Later it came back again
now with a name,
Schubert "The Youth at the Spring."
Friends called their daughter "Louisa"
also because of the song;
then it was shortened to "Lou"
ending the spell held so long.

Salzkammergut, AUSTRIA

AE VIENNA

Believing you will somehow know
if I attempt to hold
our inner transformations
I now must try;
you died before you wrote
the last of Austria.

Your elbow in the airport crowd,
tall yellow roses in the room
already bent with gold;
the grieving putto with the cross
appropriate for Mozart's plinth.
The pale green chestnuts pricked with life
among the darker boughs,
the polished globes recalling
their flickering chandeliers.
I saw you young in many dawns
beneath the leaves in prayer;
then to the Capuzinian crypt
where quiet above the Emperors' urns
the heil'ge Rita stands
for all the hopeless ones.
We drank Einspanner, strong and sweet;
above the coffee's night
soft cumulous clouds of cream
arose and sank in ravishment.

The evening blazed Schoenbrunn
and Mozart's Knabenchor.
Two hundred years the mirrors held
rococo grace in white and gold,
and now the singing boys
in periwigs and ruffled lace
and one angelic face
exquisite line of jaw.
The program changed—
Alleluia—
and all my yesterdays rushed down;
the high clear song that child I heard
beneath the chestnut in the moon
was now within the mirrored room
that once heard Mozart play.

LOOKING ON

Why is Vienna so beloved?
Her songs stay in the mind
and haunt the memory
clinging, singing, delight bringing
echoing melodies.
Elsewhere one drinks but to forget
what life and love and death can bring;
with wine Vienna praises God
life, love and death in songs
that sound beyond the night.

An Austrian poet said
one could prepare for death in life
through conscious memory,
transforming this world's wonders
forever in the mind
and so begin while still on earth
eternal verities.

No other city drinks and sings
of angels, God and Judgment Day
rejoicing, unafraid.
the treasure they were given
they seem to have within
and claim to bring their city
from this world to the next.

AUSTRIA

KREMSMUENSTER

To you was given the key
of the door in the wall
into fantasy
a white arcaded cloister
full of geometry.
Four square pools
with fountains
white arches in between
reflecting liquid dancing
and scattering parabolas
a glittering perspective
to another fairy tale.

AUSTRIA

AUSTRIA

There are inns so old on the Danube
that the Roman god of wine
is carved in stone on the lintel
upholding the centuries.

In the cloister of Heiligenkreuz
a tree and fountain are centered
easing the treadmill mind.
In the chancel the saints meditate
with brows and bones of tender wood
surrounding eyes at peace.
Cistercian monks of silence
whose voices only sing
release Gregorian chant.

Through Guiliano's cloister
where Christ the servant kneels
to wash St. Peter's feet
the monks retire
with faces carved in dignity
their white robed silence
changing
into stone.

AUSTRIA

RIVER HOUSES

Engulfed below the restless stream
rectangular reflections
are gold stability
the only permanence.
The drowning houses hold
against the water's pull
through diving arcs of swallow wings
and stay.

Ischl, AUSTRIA

TRAUENSTEIN

There quality of time
was filtered through the light
refracted from the stone
whose mountains gold at noon
would slide into the lake
throughout the afternoon.
At evening knife
they glinted rose
to flower hour on hour
above the watered dark
then through the night
they caught the stars
in stainless steel.

AUSTRIA

TALLAHASSEE

REQUIEM

All that we love and celebrate
can be transformed within
and thus abide forever
so Rilke said and we believed
but now the devastating days
are hammering your death.
I hear your birds and see
the morning hit the pool
beneath the surface sunlight flings
a dazzling of curves
becoming waves upon the shore
instead of light on stone.
Cool pines above reflecting
the glittering arabesque
the interpenetration
of water into air.

We saw between white arches
four pools where fountains rose
and threw the liquid dancing
upon the cloistered walls,
Kremsmuenster is within.

TALLAHASSEE

INSOMNIA

Night no sleep
music falls
in a well
pulling all along
sticks and stones
slip aside
leaving only sound
stilling sense
at last

NIGHT

Let suddenly rise
a morning lark
soaring the dark
dripping dew
as never when
or once upon
in Dante or in Sussex long ago;
its absence leaves
a longing there
an ache along the bone
waking again
in darkness alone.

TALLAHASSEE

ATTEMPTS AT CONSOLATION

Against the wreckful siege
of battering days
a hanging basket spills
a sudden grace
of flowers
flowing down
to leave a dazzle there
of incandescent air

Five egrets are threaded
white beads on a bough
while gulls are out wheeling
ellipses of evening
reflecting   reflecting
inversions

THE MAGIC FLUTE

The spider threads of rain
slide through begonia leaves
to Mozart's "Magic Flute"
rose petals correspond
to subtleties of sound.

A silver green Watteau
with shadows numerous
and slits of light and flute
in perilous nuance
suggesting loving death
of moonlit shattered night.

The music cascades on
enchanting every sense
the silken threads of rain
and laughter somewhere else

TALLAHASSEE

SPIDER WEB

Perhaps
    the thought
        of lace
           arose
while watching
    spider webs
        like this
           suspended
        in mist
attached
    to no apparent
        leaf
           but by itself
and pricked
    with rain
        In Bruges
           they still weave
        lace
    in thread
almost as fine
    but this is
        curved
           in space
as Einstein said

TALLAHASSEE

SUMMONS

Told to meet at station
face so long unseen
searching searching searching
anxious questioning
other exits later trains
unaware that death
had undone so many.
Eliot used the Dante line
for a crowd like this
morning breaking in
searching still in dream to see
face now well recalled.
I was told to come.

TALLAHASSEE

MANOR FARM WITHIN

Distil from tears at 3 am
whose ears will never hear
the willow wrens
whose dew fall songs
descend

The sixteenth century built the wall
left holes for seeds and planted there
the purple plume of falling hair
aubretia.
They used the lawn for bowling then
the surface was a pool
the silk of dawn across
so barefoot cool in endless May
but will they see the tracks and ask?
Long before the breakfast gong
the feet had gone.

In other centuries
long lives were led
around one place;
they saw or did not see
the cherry trees with lifted boughs
sail on a primrose sea.

Long grass is bruised with knees
the baskets are too coarse
then line them first with primrose leaves
to hold the gentle flowers.
Feel through cool grass for fragile stems
that curtsey as they fall
so tired of picking now.
Across our hands the wings of birds
the willow wrens
whose dew fall songs
descend

TALLAHASSEE

A SONG OF WILLOW

Words in other languages
birds and trains whose echoes
hollow out the sound
varying the light
adding changing nuance.

Comme c'est triste de voir s'enfuir les hirondelles

how sad it is to see the swallows fly away.
lost the sense of height
looking up in French
from the vowel turn.

Die Blaetter fallen, fallen wie von weit

the leaves are falling, falling as from far
Lost the weight of Rilke's end
finality of fall.

Dante uses Virgil's line
meeting his young love again
Purgatorio
writes her eyes are still as green
as in Florence long ago
feels

antiqua fiamma

ancient flame
This is Dido's line
leading to her pain
Purcell knew
wrote "Remember me."

Shakespeare too who put
willow in her hand
weeping for her grief
gave to Desdemona
woman scorned again
a song of willow.

Verdi's aria

Salce, salce
willow, willow
German *Weide, Weide*

heartache of lament
not quite
a song of willow.

TALLAHASSEE

HAIKU FROM TALLAHASSEE AND ELSEWHERE

Gold oak angled bridge
empty evening trees invert
a reflected theme

Chopin reverie
meandering over stones
perilously sharp

why should apple peel
wind in between blades of steel
in a northern sea

K.C.W. ROSARIAN

Bare feet along the cooling grass
are wearing their own trail
to water many roses
a heavy task
repeated endlessly
for graceful beneficiaries
who transform everyday
into early dawn
so light for them.

To spray at 5 am
for spidermites
before a working day
is chivalry to roses.
In black night and curving light
and splashing spray and steam
the roses dance exultantly
surfers in the stream
so light for them.

TALLAHASSEE

ECHO BLOWING

A folk song hauls a memory
another tongue
another land
an overwhelming past
subdues the nothing now

There once was mountain night
with lights along the lake
out in the watered dark
a melody was heard
a trumpet or a horn
and then an echo played
so long   so long   so long
it held all still
from boats far out the calls were heard
the echoes blowing through the night.

The song recalls a wood horn
an echo sounds again
from mountain night to now
so long   so long   so long

TALLAHASSEE

WINE COUNTRY

Line of mountains in the air
lapped with curling foam
slithering to blue
cypress perpendicular
champagne Codornui;
threads of vines now stitching
skeins across the hills
dancing loving arabesques
as in Limbourg manuscripts
centuries ago

SAN FRANCISCO

Streets with mountains up above
race down to sails and sea
houses crumbled bits of cheese
sprinkled through the hills
hidden now in fog
then in glancing light
snatching glitter from the sails
chinks of white;
soon the coastal range
cracked with snow
battlements of ice
hanging on to light
echoes of the houses
round the bay.

TALLAHASSEE

THE TEMPLE VASE

Encised by diamond
glass fuchsias trail
thin stamens carved in ice
which end in water drops
a luminescent spiralling
around transparency
it stands alone
a crystal vase
of England

BRADFORD PEAR

Even in the darkness it is red
that gives this tree dimension.
By day the tree is apricot,
by night it still is red
penetrating darkness
with palpability.
A light from far away
strips dim from dark below
but darkness cannot quench this tree
radiating red
irreducibly.

TALLAHASSEE

OCTOBER

Enscrolled in antique whorls
the autumn leaves
of apricot and flame
rose gold and burgundy
the wines of all the world
distill their hues
to falling flares
beyond a pane of rain
unable to subdue
the brilliance of their death

ORCHESTRA

Flutes are parallel,
diagonals oppose
rows of bows
slicing the cellos,
carving the curves
amber and rose,
transcendent wood
shining like brass,
hands above weaving
echo counterpoint.

TALLAHASSEE

CONCERTO

Strings aslant to presto
faces lost with only bows
sliding through the petalled bough
how to hold despair
batwing piano crouching there
grinning teeth devour
hummingbirds of hands
fingers hold the power
after countless years
half an hour

CELLOS

Strawberry roan or chestnut brown
maple syrup flow
what are the cello shades?
Rumps of horses gleamed like this
assured in pride of place;
even shadows are the same
down curving wood or shining flank
darkened gold to walnut warmth.
Where have all the horses gone
once a part of life?
Cellos took their shades
shapes now rarely glimpsed
metamorphosis.

TALLAHASSEE

OPERA ON RADIO AT NIGHT

A brilliant sword
a tenor voice
whose flashing edge
illuminates
obscurity
then all is dark and tense
until it sound again
may it be soon

ANALOGY

Spider rigging in the fog
knotted by the rain
with a spectral ship below
creating phantom waves
spun in morning mist
vanishing away

KREMSMUENTER REMEMBERED

Two thousand years since Virgil saw
how water in a brazen bowl
sent leaping light around the hall;
he would have smiled to see
that pool geometry
reflecting high parabolas.

TALLAHASSEE

GO OUT AT NIGHT

At night through glass the branches rise
defined against blue air
the leaves subdued
yet lured to light afar
which throws a chink to some
and leaves the rest in shade.
Go out
cool pennants of white petals loom
through curving arcs of leaves
the wings of sleeping birds unseen
all flowers smouldering
beneath the dark
the red aware of power

SASANQUA CAMELLIAS

The dark is full of stars
that are not stars
deluding the eyes
athirst for stars
in clear cold skies
yet still they soothe
compelling from the moon
a borrowed light
to shine at night

TALLAHASSEE

IN MEMORIAM FOR MY SISTER

No flowers
for one who spent her life
in growing them

No flowers
the Cancer Ward would benefit

No flowers
I should have sent
regardless
a cyclamen
to wing your way

FOR JULIE

The quantum theory could perhaps
explain haphazard fate
an airplane crash
a cancer gene
a suicide
electron swerve or lapse
not willed conceivable
among contingencies
of particles aswarm
within surreal laws

the thrusting wedge of flight
honed by migrating birds

TALLAHASSEE

DISTORTION

Brandy eases night
white camellias loom
burnishing the air
wearied with the weight of light
borrowed from the moon

Aquarium of night
with underwater leaves
unfocused falling down
through different depths of light
and one exquisite bloom
of shell and pearl and white
mosaic of the moon

Deceiving night
the petals are too small
to form so huge a sphere
there must be many flowers there
to carve in shade and light
a mirage of the moon

OLYMPIC GYMNASTS

Like kites or shredded paper
or seeds of sycamores
but not of weight and bone
the girls thrust up in air
as if on wings
like butterflies
flung out by cruel winds
the years of discipline
that gave them grace
but robbed their youth.
A phantom child forgot routine
a callous voice announced
"Her life is over now"
at seventeen
for China.

TALLAHASSEE

FORCES

Butterflies migrate
battling hurricanes
phantom wings
amber ruby gold
flowers of an hour
petals in the wind
fighting charging cloud
overwhelming odds
yet some do arrive.

BY CHANCE

By chance
the random light
will snatch a certain branch
and fling it forward
all in gold
against the coming dark
until a sudden cloud
subdues the flame
like laughter
as quickly as it came

TALLAHASSEE